Hollywood loves Tom Cruise. His movies aren't all very good, but they always make money. Tom is a success. But there are problems, too. At work, Tom is sometimes difficult. In love, he is sometimes unhappy. He is often angry at newspaper stories about him. Why is this? Some of the answers are in Tom's early years. His story is interesting. It is the story of a star.

Barcode at back →

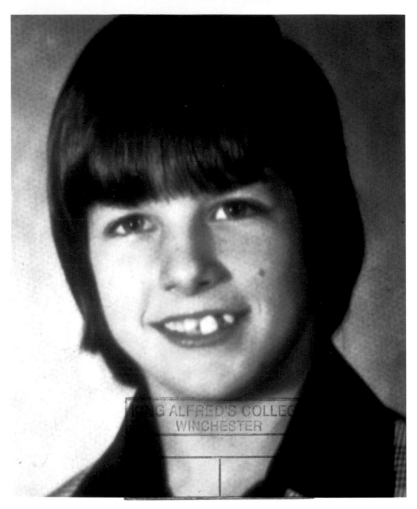

On July 3, 1962, in Syracuse, New York, the Mapother family have their first son. His name is Thomas Cruise Mapother and they call him Tom.

In the photo, young Tom has a happy smile. But the family move seven times in eleven years and Tom can't make good friends. There are problems at school, too. He can't read or write very well.

Tom's mother and father divorce in 1973. In 1978, his
mother marries again and the family move to New Jersey.
At home, Tom is often unhappy about his father. But at
school, he plays games well. He is a good actor, too. Tom
is a big success in the star role in *Guys and Dolls*.
"This is the right job for me," he thinks. "But it's the
wrong place. New York is the place for young actors."

Tom moves to New York in July, 1980, but there aren't many jobs for new actors.

"Try an agent," his mother says. Tom finds an agent. Later that year, he finds some work in movies, but only small roles. Then, in 1981, director Howard Becker is looking for an angry young soldier for his action movie, *Taps*. Tom gets the job.

Taps is a big success for Tom. After this, he is in five movies in three years.

In 1986, he has the star role in *Top Gun*. It is an action movie about a pilot in a US military school. Tom plays the role of Pete "Maverick" Mitchell, their number one student. *Top Gun* is the movie of the year in the US. It makes $177,000,000 and it makes Tom Cruise a big star.

Tom's girlfriend at this time is the actress, Mimi Rogers.
In May, 1987, they marry. Later that year, Tom stars
with Paul Newman in *The Color of Money*.

In 1988, he is in *Rain Man* with Dustin Hoffman. It is not
an action movie and some newspapers are unhappy about
this. "Tom's fans only want action movies," they say. They
are wrong. *Rain Man* is the year's number one movie.

For *Born on the Fourth of July* (1989), Tom gets a
Golden Globe★ award. He is famous, but there are
problems at work. "Write that scene again," he says.
Mimi has problems, too. "To many people I am only
Mrs. Tom Cruise," she says. They divorce and Tom finds
new love with the Australian actress, Nicole Kidman.

★Golden Globe: Newspaper people give this award to actors.

Tom and Nicole star in the 1990 movie, *Days of Thunder*. They marry on December 24. After this, Tom stops work for some months and takes vacations with Nicole.

He starts work again in 1991. He and Nicole are in the movie *Far and Away*, but it is not a big success. A year later, Tom is in *A Few Good Men* with Jack Nicholson and Demi Moore. The movie makes $102,000,000.

Tom wants a family. He and Nicole can't have children,
but in 1993 they adopt a girl, Isabella. Two years later,
they adopt a boy, Connor.

Tom's big movies of the years 1993 to 1996 are *The Firm*,
Interview With a Vampire, and *Mission Impossible*. In
Mission Impossible he has two jobs, producer and actor.
He plays an American military agent.

In *Jerry Maguire* (1996), Tom plays the star role very well. "Can he get an Oscar★?" the newspapers ask. The answer is no, but Tom gets another Golden Globe award.

Tom is often angry with the newspapers. Sometimes, they visit his family and friends and ask questions about his early years. Often, the stories about him are wrong.

★Oscar: A Hollywood award for a very good actor.

In 1997, the famous director, Stanley Kubrick, wants Tom and Nicole for his new movie. The two actors like his work. They make *Eyes Wide Shut* in England for a year. "The movie is all about love scenes," some newspapers say. "They are wrong," Tom and Nicole answer.

Tom and Nicole go to the premiere and they are happy with their roles in the movie.

Usually, a movie has one story, but there are nine stories in Tom's 1999 movie, *Magnolia*. Tom is only in one of them. In the movie, he teaches men about women. Tom has success in this role. He has success away from the movie, too. He gets another Golden Globe award.

One year later, he and the famous British actor, Anthony Hopkins, star in *Mission Impossible 2*.

It is the year 2000. Things are good for Tom and Nicole.
They have two beautiful children. They work with
famous directors. They have expensive cars, airplanes, a
big boat, and homes in the United States and Australia.
They have a big house in London, too. Movie stars are
often unhappy in love. "But," people say, "Tom Cruise
has a happy family."

But Tom and Nicole are often unhappy. For Tom, home
is always the United States. "He's an American boy,"
Nicole says. "For me, Australia is very important."
There are problems with work, too. Tom and Nicole
don't work in the same place very often. Sometimes,
they don't meet for weeks. Tom is very unhappy about
all this. Early in 2001, he asks for a divorce.

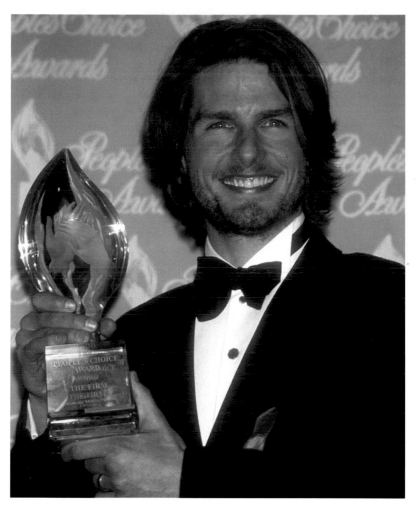

"He's happy at work and happy in love," people say of Tom Cruise in the 1990s. Now they don't say this. Today, Tom isn't only a young action star with a friendly smile and a happy family. In his work, he plays many roles and he plays all of them well. This makes him interesting. Only one man can make good movies *and* bad movies into successes. His name is Tom Cruise.

ACTIVITIES

Before you read

1 Answer the questions.

   a Where is Tom Cruise from?

   b Why is he the number one actor in Hollywood?

   c Can you name five of his movies?

2 Find the words in your dictionary.

   action   actor/actress   adopt   agent   another   award
   director   divorce   fan   many   marry   military   pilot
   premiere   producer   role   scene   soldier   star   success

   Find the words for people and their jobs.

After you read

3 Answer the questions about Tom Cruise.

   a Why is Tom sometimes angry with newspapers?

   b One movie makes Tom a big star. What is its name?

   c Name two of Tom's problems with Nicole.

   d What problems do directors sometimes have with Tom?

   e What movies are not action movies? Name two.

4 Talk about Tom Cruise. "He is Hollywood's number one movie star." Is this right? What do *you* think?

5 Write about one of Tom Cruise's movies. What is the story? What do you like about it?

Answers fo   ers titles are
       avail   te to:
Marketing   WC2R 0RL.